G000154026

Made in France

By Reed Darmon

CHRONICLE BOOKS

SAN FRANCISCO

Page 254 constitutes a continuation of the copyright page.

Library of Congress Cataloging-in-Publication Data:
Darmon, Reed.
  Made in France / by Reed Darmon.
    p. cm.
  ISBN 978-0-8118-6525-8
  1. Commercial art—France—History—20th century. 2. Graphic arts—France—History—20th century. I. Title.
NC998.6.F7D37 2009
741.60944'0904—dc22

                        2008036998

Manufactured in China

Designed by Reed Darmon

Photography by Régis Boissier, Lyon, France; Alan Borrud, Portland, Oregon; Reed Darmon, Portland, Oregon; Jean-Luc Fradet, Déols, France; and Merrill L. Mabbs, Rapid City, South Dakota.

Consultation and translations by Bernard Sampo and Dana Hoyle.

10 9 8 7 6 5 4 3 2 1

Chronicle Books LLC
680 Second Street
San Francisco, California 94107
www.chroniclebooks.com

PAGE 1: An illustration by Leonetto Cappiello on the cover of a brochure published by the Centre National d'Expansion du Tourisme in 1937.

PAGE 2: Detail of a fashion plate from the magazine *Gazette du Bon Ton* titled "The Sentimental Journey" (1922).

OPPOSITE: A box of Tokalon brand face powder, 1920s.

Dedicated to Edouard Pécourt,
le grand passionné de Tango

and Moto Hyun,
le compagnon de voyage

Introduction

In 1925 the Eiffel Tower lit up the night sky with a gigantic illuminated advertisement for Citroën cars. July of that year saw the opening of the massive trade fair Exposition Internationale des Arts Décoratifs et Industriels Modernes, with such displays as "Arts and Crafts of the Negro" and "The Ideal Apartment for a Young Couple" (this last sponsored by the department store Galeries Lafayette). It was this exhibition that established *"modernisme"* (later called Art Déco) as the look of the new century. Modern art and commercial culture were having a love affair, and France was at its heart.

After all, it was in Paris in 1907 that Picasso and Braque invented Cubism, and other art movements followed in rapid succession: Futurism, Dada, Surrealism. Within this artistic demimonde, madness had become chic, scandals were a form of publicity, and even though the economy was struggling, Paris felt like the center of the world.

^ "The board is quite short" to bridge the gulf separating France from liberty. Lithograph by Honoré Daumier in *Charivari*, 1860s.

Of course, the stage had already been set by French innovations during the nineteenth century. Honoré Daumier had pushed the limits of social satire with his scathing images in the newspaper *Charivari*, and Henri de Toulouse-Lautrec had elevated the advertising poster to a high art.

By the 1920s, Paris had become the pinnacle of urban design. From Brazil to Vietnam, the Parisian city plan was emulated as the ideal of what a twentieth-century city should look like: that combination of grand boulevards and intimate side streets that spoke of national pride, wealth, and especially cultural maturity. In a time when United States' might was taking center stage, Francophilia was the alternative to raw commercialism. It was café culture, freewheeling public discourse, respect for etiquette, and refinement in everyday dining and drinking, that distinguished the Gallic republican spirit.

Modernism flourished all over Europe and the United States, but it was in France, with its traditions of social satire and

^ A postcard of the Eiffel Tower illuminated with advertising, 1925.

sexual openness, that it gained a playful, experimental edge.

It is poignant to remember that for much of the century, France sampled U.S. popular culture as if at a buffet, the same way it appropriated ideas, music, and styles from the rest of the world (especially its own colonies). But inevitably, part of the French cultural project became a response to the American juggernaut, both admiring and critical. The explosion of sophisticated moviemaking in the 1950s and '60s, France's New Wave, exemplified the homage/attack dichotomy.

It was between the First and Second World Wars that France was at its extravagant best, and this is evident in the country's vibrant magazine culture. Even from the beginning of the century, magazines manifested the finest artistic expression in their content, but by the 1920s, costly and painstaking effort went into their production as well. Magazines like *Gazette du Bon Ton* featured elegant images imprinted on fine paper using a manual stencil technique called *pochoir*. This trend culminated in the 1930s with magazines that were art objects in their own right, such as *Verve*, established in 1937, which included actual art prints in its pages.

By then, designers and illustrators had achieved near celebrity status, and advertisers granted them the freedom to explore a product's qualities in new and abstract ways. Attitude, style itself had become the message.

France had an exceptional ability to appropriate world culture. The café music of the *accordéonistes*, so closely identified with France, blends Gypsy, Italian, and native Auvergne styles, and the great French music-hall tradition happily embraced jazz. Many black performers from the United States as well as Africa found a welcome reception in France. With the Exposition Coloniale of 1931, displaying art and culture from around the world, and the gigantic Exposition Internationale des Arts et Techniques dans la Vie Moderne of 1937, Parisians had a steady diet of internationalism between the wars.

Fashion houses, show business, and politics provided content for the great pictorial weeklies of the period until

^ An advertisement for Bonal aperitif by A. M. Cassandre, 1933.

the Nazi occupation of 1940 to 1944, when many magazines dropped away and innovative French culture was on hold. During the reconstruction period from 1945 to 1950, print and press technologies received a much needed updating, and talented designers found work with state-run agencies, creating everything from train service schedules and lottery posters to tourism brochures. In the 1950s the demands of worldwide mass-marketing, with its straight-forward branding techniques, amplified the internationalist facet of France's graphic style. But by the late 1960s, distrust of the dominant cultural message had produced a burst of graphic arts with social critique highly reminiscent of the avant-garde publications that had flourished earlier in the century.

∧ *Paris Magazine*, 1933.

It is an exhilarating project to race through a century of the popular culture, both high and low, of a country as extraordinary as France. Any collection of images can only be subjective and personal, and omissions are inevitable. As in any country with a huge and singular capital city, France's culture is dominated by its political and artistic nucleus, Paris — and so, ultimately, is this book. I have also tended to linger in the time between the wars, because the ferment of those years is irresistible. To explore French graphics is to watch the fine arts movements of the day feeding into commercial culture with a sophisti-cation unmatched anywhere in the world.

— Reed Darmon

Prix : 0,50

∧ A poster for the winter season at the Alcazar D'Hiver theater,
featuring Marie Futlais and the Futlais brothers, from around 1890.

< A playbill from the turn of the century for "La Revue de La Scala."

^ A woman reveals her knickers on the cover of the weekly
Gil Blas, the quintessential, somewhat naughty Belle Epoque
paper of opinion and satire, August 1901.

∧ In the years before World War I, the magazine *L'Assiette au Beurre,* devoted itself to radical social causes and attracted some of the most gifted graphic artists of its time. Issue number 120 was a visual essay on the subject of perfidious snobbery.

L'Assiette au Beurre took on all sorts of social topics from its critical and anarchist perspective, including state power, economic corruption, religion, and even love and sex, as in the issue at right, a cynical examination of romance, titled "What Is This?"

★ Nouvelle Série. N° 133. — 19 Août 1905.

20 centimes.

UN AN
Paris et Départements, 10 fr.
Étranger, 14 fr.

SIX MOIS
France, 5.50 — Étranger, 7.50

Félix JUVEN, Directeur
123, rue Réaumur, 123
PARIS

VENTE ET ABONNEMENTS
9, rue Saint-Joseph, 9

JOURNAL HUMORISTIQUE PARAISSANT LE SAMEDI

LES MARIS-GARÇONS

— Oh! ma chérie, c'que tu m'changes de ma femme!

Dessin d'Hermann-Paul.

^   The most successful of all the humor and satire magazines, *Le Rire*,
ran from 1894 to the 1950s. The caption on this cover from August 1905
reads: "Oh, my dear, you're such a change from my wife!"

^ *Le Sourire* was another one of the many lighthearted and slightly risqué
magazines before and after World War I. This cover titled
"En Route to Cythère" is from June 1921.

^ A classic "naughty" French postcard
showing a leotard-wearing beauty was titled
"The Woman with a Mask."

> The biting satirical magazine *Comica* had a January 1909
cover illustration titled "Deception," in which theatergoers are
disappointed that a play does not solve a celebrated murder case.

PRIX : 75 cent.   IIe Année. — No 5. Janvier 1909

Comica

" A moi le monde "

Dessin de MARTRUS (Espagne).

DÉCEPTION
— Vois-tu, maman, ce Foyer n'est pas si...... Steinheil que ça...

Enttäuschung.
— Weisst du, Mama, das "Foyer"*) ist gar nicht so "steinheilig", wie ich dachte.

Deception.
— Look here, Mamma, This play " Le Foyer ", has not so much of the celebrated murder case Steinheil, as we thought.

*) Titel eines im Theatre Français aufgeführten, als "starkes Stück" angekündigten Schauspieles.

13e Année № N°631   NUMÉRO EXCEPTIONNEL, 32 PAGES : 50 Centimes.   22 Octobre 1910. № Tous les Samedis.
(Étranger : 60 Centimes)

LA VIE AU GRAND AIR

LE SALON DE LA LOCOMOTION AÉRIENNE

ÉDITIONS PIERRE LAFITTE & Cie, 90, AVENUE DES CHAMPS-ELYSÉES, PARIS

∧ France was in the forefront of aviation in the early years of the twentieth century, and this October 1910 "outdoor life" magazine reviews an exhibition of flying machines held at the Grand Palais exhibition hall in Paris.

> This postcard was sent from the 1908 International Exposition of Electricity held in Marseille, using its official postage stamp, below.

21

^ > *La Vie Parisienne*, a popular, somewhat erotic literary and humor
magazine, played a part in Paris's reputation as a city of risqué tastes.
But during World War I it could also be very patriotic.
These issues are from 1916 (above) and 1917 (opposite).

LA VIE PARISIENNE

LA PREMIÈRE HIRONDELLE

∧ During World War I, the bayonet was nicknamed "Rosalie" and was personified as a female patriot. In this special issue of *La Baïonnette* she is brandishing her namesake as the mighty pen.

> Issues of the newspapers *Le Matin* and *Le Journal* from June and July 1919, announcing the end of World War I and the return of the victorious troops to Paris.

Cᵗᵉ Gᵗᵉ TRANSATLANTIQUE

CHEMIN DE FER D'ORLEANS

LE MAROC

Via BORDEAUX

< ∧ Two postcards based on posters from around 1910 advertising train travel on the *chemin de fer,* or "ribbon of steel": Western France (opposite), and Morocco with connections in Bordeaux (above).

Art Nouveau labels on two brands of soap (right and below right) and a brand of cologne (below left) from the early twentieth century.

IDÉAL

PAUL TRANOY

SAVONNERI

EAU

DE

COLOGNE

TRIPLE SUPÉRIEURE

Nᵒ 156

Savon
Bouquet
Française Hygiénique
Paris
830

Savon
Extra-Fin
PARFUMERIE
ERIZMA
Paris

Art Déco labels on packages of soap (above and right top)
and a bottle of cologne (right bottom) from the 1920s.

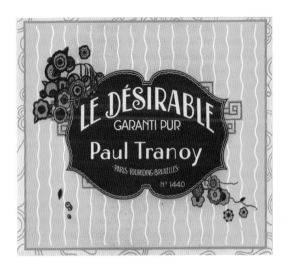

LE DÉSIRABLE
GARANTI PUR
Paul Tranoy
·PARIS·TOURCOING·BRUXELLES·
N° 1440

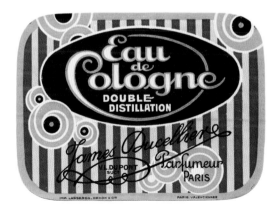

Eau de Cologne
DOUBLE-DISTILLATION
James Ducellier
V.L.DUPONT SUCr
Parfumeur
PARIS

^ > Labels on packages of soap from
around 1925, by unknown designers.

SAVON
MIMOSA
unico
n° 55

CHAQUE
SAVONNETTE
DONNE DROIT
À UN **TICKET-PRIME**

The art of advertising fans flourished in France as early as 1910, and the liquor industry especially took advantage of these handheld fluttering ads. Here are promotions for Veramint de Ricqlès Liqueur (left), Sorin Cognac (below), and Le Curaçao by Picon (right).

✔ A fan advertising the products available from Suchard Chocolates and Cocoa, illustrated by an unknown artist in the 1920s.

^ A small Déco purse from the 1920s
made with tiny metal beads.

PARAPLUIE-REVEL

Cappiello 1922

^ This lithographed postcard version of the famous poster
by influential illustrator Leonetto Cappiello, advertising
Revel brand umbrellas, was printed in 1922.

> A poster for Blue Rice brand cigarette rolling paper.

PAPIER A CIGARETTES

RIZ BLEU
CHARLES LACROIX
ANGOULÊME

BUVARD EXTRA
A CONSERVER

LE THERMOGÈNE

COMBAT { Toux, Grippe
Douleurs Rhumatismales

∧ This version of the famous ad, created by the prolific illustrator Leonetto Cappiello, for Le Thermogène, a cotton wadding treatment for "coughs, colds, pain, rheumatism," appears on a sheet of blotter paper.

＞ "The Discovery of Athletes," states this ad for a muscle liniment called Chanteclair, which "soothes, fortifies, electrifies."

LE
RÉVÉLATEUR
DES ATHLÈTES

L'EMBROCATION
CHANTECLAIR
ASSOUPLIT. FORTIFIE. ÉLECTRISE

LABORATOIRE FURNON
SAINTE SIGOLÈNE (HAUTE LOIRE)

^ The publication *Gazette du Bon Ton*, meaning "timeless good taste," was France's most exclusive fashion magazine during its run from 1912 to 1925 and was printed on fine paper, often using a laborious printing technique called *pochoir*, in which colors were hand applied using stencils. Many of the top fashion illustrators, pioneers of Déco style, were featured. Above is the cover for the summer issue for 1923.

> A plate from a *Gazette du Bon Ton*, 1920 titled "The Promenade at Montmartre," illustrated by Charles Martin with fashion by de Beer.

DIANE

∧ A plate from a 1920 *Gazette du Bon Ton* titled "Diane" featured a design for Max Furriers drawn by E. G. Benito.

> A plate from 1920, "The Porcelain Hat," was styled by Torquate and drawn by Charles Martin.

^ This 1920s pochoir plate called "Morning Dress"
from *Costumes Parisiens,* shows a man passing the book
and print vendors that lined the Seine river in Paris exactly
as they do today, and from whom prints such as this one
can still be purchased.

^ This cover of *Monsieur*, a magazine of men's fashion and opinion, from October 1922, is a fine pochoir print with artwork by Jacques François.

L'Orgueil

^ This pochoir plate from 1924 is titled "Arrogance."

ANTINÉA

Manteau du soir, de Paul Poiret

∧ Paul Poiret, the most influential fashion designer of his time, the master of Déco and Orientalist fashion, designed this evening coat seen in the April 1920 issue of *Gazette du Bon Ton*.

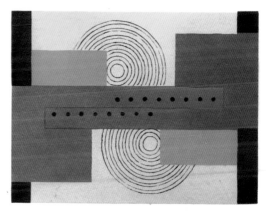

∧ Two tapestry patterns by Silva Bruhns from a
luxuriously printed series of portfolios titled *Répertoire
du Goût Moderne* (Compendium of Modern Taste)
printed in Paris from 1928 to 1929.

< A page of "Inspirations" from a folio of stencil-printed Modernist patterns.

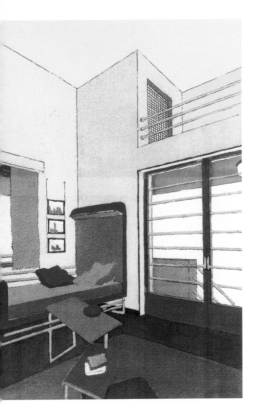

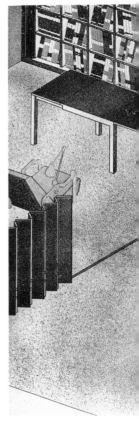

52

◄ ∧ Two pages from *Répertoire du Goût Moderne*, Editions Albert Lévy, 1929, finely printed using silver ink, show how industrial design and new kinds of materials, including steel tubing and Bakelite plastic, had become stylish elements in domestic interiors for a new age. At left, a bedroom; above, an office with a library.

∧ > Two pochoir illustrations of domestic furnishings from *Répertoire du Goût Moderne*; a group of ceiling light fixtures designed by Francis Jourdain (above) and dinnerware designed by Jean Luce (opposite). This style, originally called Art Moderne, eventually became known worldwide as Art Déco.

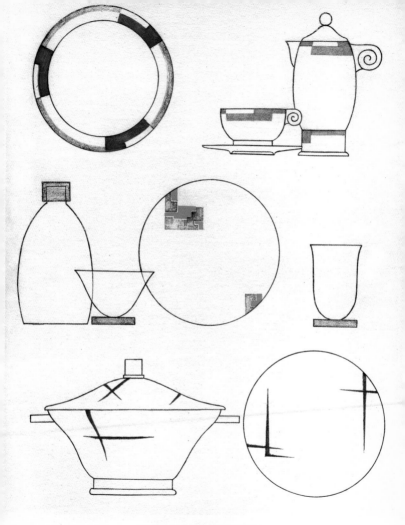

CÉRAMIQUE ET VERRERIE DE TABLE
par JEAN LUCE

< A page from *Répertoire du Goût Moderne* showing pieces of furniture for a children's room shaped like vowels and the letters *M* and *G*, designed by J. Adnet.

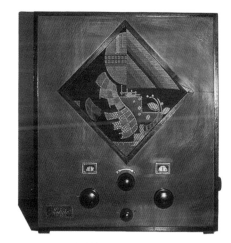

^ A tabletop radio by Radiola, 1932, features a striking Art Déco grill cloth.

< This electromagnetic speaker from Gaumont Lumière, 1925, displays an elegant contrast between the metal frame and the pleated paper diaphragm.

^ "How the French Imagine New York," a drawing by Zyg Brunner
from *Gazette du Bon Ton* No. 2, 1923.

∧ *Music-Hall*, 1935, a program for the First International Festival of Music-Hall, which took place at the Alhambra theater and featured singer Mathea Merriefield.

> *La Rampe,* a magazine of theater, music, and film, 1932, features two stars of the movie *Monsieur de Pourceaugnac*, which was based on a play by Molière.

^ Le Théâtre des Bouffes Parisiens presents two comedies in this playbill from around 1913 with a cover by influential illustrator George Barbier.

> A playbill for Casino de Paris' 1929 revue *Paris-Miss*, with an illustration on the cover by Frisco, one of the production's costume designers.

< *Revenez-y . . . !*, a play in three acts, was presented at Ba-Ta-Clan in 1925 with this playbill illustrated by Barjansky.

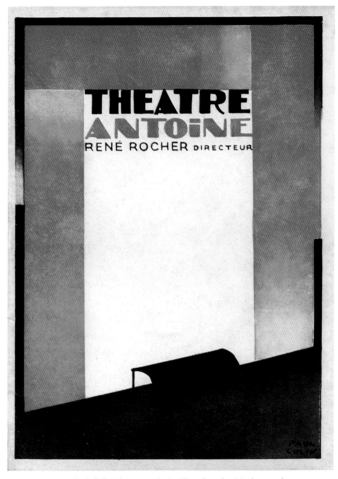

^ A playbill for the comedy *Le Plancher des Vaches* at the
Théâtre Antoine's 1931 season, with a cover design by Paul Colin.

^ A playbill for the musical comedy *Le Bonheur, Mesdames!*
at the Théâtre Marigny, 1934, with a cover design by "Don."

^ A souvenir album for the Casino de Paris Revue *Tout Paris* from 1928, lavishly printed by Editions Artistiques de Paris. The Casino de Paris was famous at the time for its spectacular production numbers and enormous cast.

^ This cover of *Paris Plaisirs,* an entertainment and theater
magazine, features the Irvin Sisters, who were performing
at the legendary Moulin Rouge in May 1926.

ABONNEMENTS
UN AN
France et Colonies 40 fr.
Étranger . . . . . 75 fr.

Chèques Postaux Paris 1622.38
R. C. Seine 248.570 B

RÉDACTION
ADMINISTRATION
PUBLICITÉ
227, RUE SAINT-DENIS
PARIS (2e)

Téléphone { GUTENBERG 16-04
            { CENTRAL 49-07

NUMÉRO 18

FÉVRIER 1933

REVUE MENSUELLE

Studio PIAZ

Joséphine BAKER

L'HABIT NE FAIT PAS LE MOINE...

PARAIT LE MERCREDI

VU
JOURNAL DE LA SEMAINE
65-67 Avenue des Champs-Élysées, Paris (VIIIe). Tel. Élysées 27-57

LIRE DANS
CE NUMÉRO :

LES MAITRES
DE L'OPINION
N° 2
M. CH. MAURRAS
CO-DIRECTEUR
DE «L'ACTION
FRANÇAISE»

LE LIDO VÉNITIEN

LE SIONISME
EN PALESTINE

LE MOULAGE DES
FIGURES VIVANTES

AU REVOIR BLACK BIRDS !

L'étonnante troupe des Chocolate Kiddies et son étoile Adelaïde Hall, après avoir ravi
Paris pendant de longs mois, s'envolent. Et le Moulin-Rouge fermera ses plus
spélébres pour devenir un cinéma. Adieu Moulin-Rouge ! Au revoir Black Birds !

PHOTO GERMAINE KRULL

N°77 - 4 SEPTEMBRE 1929   PRIX : 1 FR. 50

^ Black entertainers enjoyed high status in France early in
the twentieth century. On this cover of the pictorial weekly *VU*
for September 1929, the headline plays on the song "Bye Bye
Black Birds" to announce that a Moulin Rouge star performer,
Adelaide Hall, has left for a career in cinema.

< The title page of the February 1933 *Paris Magazine*, a review of
entertainment, featured the extraordinary American expatriate Josephine
Baker, who was by then the lead act at the Folies Bergère, a film and
record star, a force in fashion, and a pioneer of black visibility.

^ A store-window ad for Visseaux brand
radio tubes: a "Mark of Progress."

^ "You will no longer need to wind up your clocks, they will run on electricity!" reads this window card advertising Vedette brand electric clocks.

< A box camera called the Eclair Lux was made by the Tiranty company.

^ This placard advertising Alfa brand cigarette paper, with a sample package attached, states that it "rolls so much better."

> A bookmark advertising Gitanes cigarettes, designed by René Vincent around 1935.

∧ This version of the story *Beauty and the Beast*, illustrated by
Lucienne Loyeux, was printed in Paris for Hachette books in the 1920s.

^ The fourth book of adventures of the fearless monkey, Zozo,
written and illustrated by C. Franchi for Editions Touret, 1936.

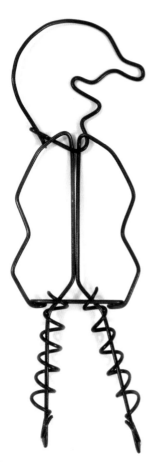

< ∧ This novelty item required
carefully unfolding to reveal *My Cousin
Tireliboudin* or "wire drawing."
The box reads "Lift up his head,
don't lose yours"

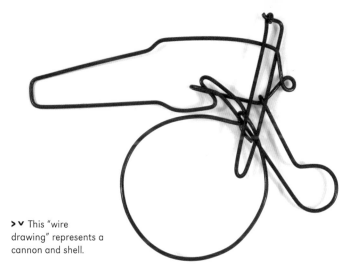

> ❯ ❮ This "wire drawing" represents a cannon and shell.

LE FILON D'OR

PAR JACQUES ANGIOUX

N° 17 · COLLECTION *Printemps* · 50c

< American Indians capture a group of scouts in this page-turner from the Spring Collection of "Adventure Novels for the Young," printed in Paris in the 1920s.

> An African guide comes to the rescue of three boy scouts in this novel by Jean de La Hire for J. Férenczi books, 1920.

Les Trois Boy-Scouts

par Jean de LA HIRE

Georges Vallée

35 c. LE VOLUME COMPLET

J. FÉRENCZI, Éditeur, 9, Rue Antoine Chantin. PARIS. 14e

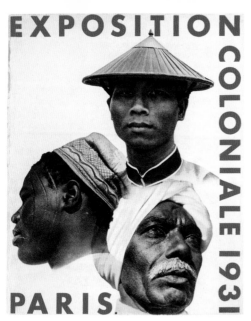

EXPOSITION COLONIALE 1931

PARIS.

In 1931, France could boast of colonial holdings around the world. The gigantic Exposition Coloniale of that year featured art exhibits and mock villages from Asia, Africa, and the Middle East.

^ A portfolio of photographs from an exhibition by M. Cloche, finely printed by Studio Deberny Peignot.
> A postcard for English-speaking visitors to the Exposition Coloniale.

INTERNATIONAL OVERSEAS EXHIBITION

ROUND THE WORLD IN ONE DAY

PARIS 1931

∧ The May 1931 issue of the satire magazine *Le Rire*, for which
nothing was sacred, makes fun of the exotic sights and
baffled crowds at the Exposition Coloniale.

PARIS 1937
EXPOSITION INTERNATIONALE

ART ET TECHNIQUES
DANS LA VIE MODERNE

The International Exposition of Art and Technology in Modern Life, 1937, was a spectacular gathering of design and scientific innovation as well as a flashpoint of political tension. The Nazi and Soviet pavilions faced each other, and Picasso's painting "Guernica" depicted the horrors of the Spanish Civil War.

< A flyer designed by Villemot and Bouissoud.

> A special edition of the arts magazine *L'Illustration* for the exposition.

L'ILLUSTRATION

EXPOSITION PARIS 1937

DESSIN DE A. BRENET

ALBUM HORS SÉRIE

PRIX : 20 F™

L'Officiel

DE LA
COUTURE
DE LA
MODE
DE PARIS

Madame Le Monnier

^ This issue of the fashion magazine *L'Officiel* for February 1930
featured society women modeling the season's fashions.

Satin
Peau d'Ange

Ruban
lingerie lavable
en satin envers crêpe
ruban & coloris déposés

^ An ad for Ruban Lingerie in *L'Officiel* achieved
a high Déco effect using silver ink in 1930.

femina

CHAPEAUX D'AUTOMNE ET
PREMIÈRES ROBES D'HIVER

^ In the years before photography came to dominate magazines, illustrators were free to create stylized visions of glamour. This cover of fashion magazine *Femina* was illustrated by Weclawowicz.

< This *Vogue* from November 1928 is devoted to fashion for the coming winter. The rigorously modern cover is by an unknown artist.

SUCCURSALE DE LUXE
DE LA SAMARITAINE
27, BOULEVARD DES CAPUCINES PARIS

∧ A sterling silver Déco cigarette case by an unknown manufacturer.

‹ Fine embossed printing is featured on this brochure for the deluxe salesrooms of the Samaritaine department store.

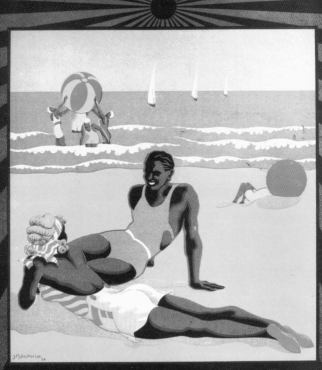

BRUNI - PLAGE

Agréablement parfumé

Assouplit la peau et la bronze tout
en la protégeant des coups de soleil

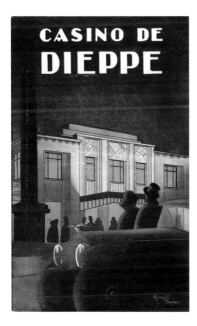

‹ Two brochures for travel to the beach: the Casino de Dieppe on the Atlantic coast in Normandy (left), and Cannes with "The most beautiful beach and finest sand on the Côte d'Azur," on the Mediterranean (below).

‹ A store window sign for "Tan-Beach" lotion states that it is pleasantly perfumed, softens and tans skin and protects from sunburn.

LE SOLEIL
LA MER
LA PLUS BRIL-
LANTE SAISON
ARTISTIQUE
ET SPORTIVE
DU MONDE

MONTE CARLO

LE JOYAU DE LA CÔTE D'AZUR

HAVAS

∧ > Two magazine ads from the early 1930s for Monte Carlo on France's Côte d'Azur: "The sun, the sea, the most brilliant artistic and sports season in the world" (above) and "Summer in Monte Carlo Beach. It's the sun, the sun . . . ," (right).

RÉALISEZ VOTRE RÊVE DE SOLEIL...

VISITEZ
L'ESPAGNE

∧ Along with trains and ocean liners, cars became icons of
speed in the machine age, as in this 1932 ad for the French
car manufacturer Panhard, illustrated by Alexis Kow.

‹ "Realize your dream of sun. Visit Spain," says this
magazine ad from the 1930s, designed by Pierre Leconte.

CADEAUX

A LA GRANDE MAISON DE BLANC

PLACE de l'OPERA
PARIS

TOLMER

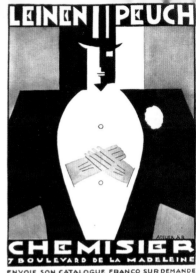

LEINEN PEUCH

CHEMISIER
7 BOULEVARD DE LA MADELEINE
ENVOIE SON CATALOGUE FRANCO SUR DEMANDE

ATELIER A.B.

NICOLAS

EXPOSITION DE CADEAUX
ENTRÉE LIBRE

MERCIER
FRÈRES
100, Faub St-Antoine - 77, Champs-Elysées

AU GIRARD

LE PÉTROLE HAHN

ARRÊTE LA CHUTE DES CHEVEUX

Artistic breakthoughs in Paris in the 1920s and '30s along with a sophisticated popular culture, established modernism as *the* essential look in advertising. The limited availability of color posed no obstacle to graphic experimentation. These early 1930s ads are from *L'Illustration* and *Vogue*.

UN **DUBONNET**

vin tonique au quinquina

< > French advertising between World Wars I and II lead the world in its balance of sophisticated playfulness. The makers of Dubonnet, an aperitif, used the top designers of the day to create their identity with that spirit, including Leonetto Cappiello (left) and Adolphe Mouron Cassandre (right).

Revillon

PARIS

< An advertisement for Revillon cosmetics by Paul Colin, an influential designer during the French Jazz Age.

> Two examples of early color photography in advertising: Rivoire & Carret, a pasta company (above) and Mossant, makers of the "Scottish" hat (right).

MON
ƒEUL
AMI

PARFUM **isabey**

26, FAUBOURG S^T HONORÉ PARIS
A. LANG

^ The Parisian transplant and celebrity artist Tsuguharu
Foujita applied a Japanese sensibility in this illustration
for the perfume "My Only Friend" by Isabey.

> With its elegant images and metallic inks, this edition
of the magazine *L'Illustration*, edited by René Baschet for
Christmas 1940, envisions a magazine as a fine art object.

L'ILLUSTRATION

NOËL 1940

> An advertisment from 1930 states "Coty down to the fingertips."

∧ > The hugely successful perfume house founded by François Coty in 1904 pioneered package design and the department store perfume counter. Coty continued to exploit its Parisian image (right) long after its move to New York City.

vous êtes ravissante mais son coeur dort
encore — attendez! — Un parfum de Lenthéric —
impérieux et vibrant — sera comme une sirène
— le coeur s'éveillera en bondissant !

Lenthéric PARIS
Ses Parfums

< This ad for Lenthéric perfume states that though you are beautiful, his heart still sleeps, until a Lenthéric scent—imperious and vibrant—like a siren song, makes it leap.

> Labels on affordable colognes from the 1930s.

Three bars of French soap: Lanoline Soap by Vibert Brothers, Cold Cream soap by Chomé, and Dulcia Beauty Soap by Cheramy.

Two scent cards for L.T. Piver perfumes: "Dream of Gold," (above) and "Devilries" (right).

DIABLERIES

L.T. PIVER

PARIS

< A package of L'Oréal Shampoo powder from the 1940s.

^ > Ricinol brand brilliantine will "shine and revive the hair."

^ A package of The Rooster extra-thin razor blades and a single patented Aramis razor blade.

^ A tube of Roja brand brilliantine for men from the laboratories of Dr. Roja, established 1907.

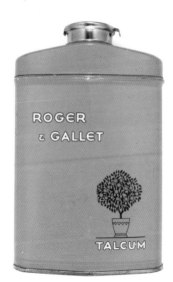

> A tin of talcum powder from Roger & Gallet, 1940s.

^ A tin of Banania brand Breakfast Chocolate drink. The image is of a Senegalese infantryman saying "It is good" in a sort of pidgin French.

∨ A tin of sweets from Pierrot Gourmand, Paris. The character Pierrot is a French version of an old Commedia Dell'Arte clown.

< A tin of Partridge Licorice: "It's the best."

^ A bar of Granetias brand chocolate, from the 1940s.

^ A package of Honey-Licorice sweets from John Tavernier, made from "pure honey."

> "I drink Blécao to the health of my Emperor," states this advertising card for a hot beverage for young people.

Découper les contours de l'image.

JE BOIS DU **BLÉCAO**
À LA SANTÉ DE MON EMPEREUR

^ Wrappers for a bar of milk chocolate (top) and a bar of
a sugar-cream confection (above) from Fraiture Brother and Sister.

VIEILLE FINE

SPIRITUEUX MAISON J. DESMET-MAERTENS
MENENSTEENWEG-163-RUMBEKE
R.C. COURTRAI 13491 • TEL. 051-20653 • CONT. 0,18 - 0,48 - 0,70 - 0,97 L.

SIROP DE GRENADINE

PUR SUCRE

> Labels for Spiritueux aged liqueur (top) and for a bottle of Grenadine Syrup from Fère-Champenoise (bottom).

^ A poster for Duval-Leroy Champagne from the town of
Epernay in the Marne region of northern France.

VIN DE FRUITS BLANC

Garanti de fruits frais

R. C. COURTRAI 13.491

Si vous aimez un vin
distingué, bouqueté,
fruité, à la fois léger
et corsé, réclamez le

FONT DU ROY

ROUGE · BLANC · ROSE

à votre fournisseur habituel

∧ A label for white wine, "guaranteed fresh."
< An ad for Font du Roy wines says, "If you like a distinguished wine with a fruity bouquet, at the same time light and full bodied, ask for Font du Roy, red, white, and rosé."

117

HUILE LESIEUR
POUR LA TABLE
UNE SEULE QUALITÉ : LA MEILLEURE !!

^ "The Best!!" An ad for Lesieur salad oil
for the table, illustrated by Henry Monnier.

> A poster for Faucon duck pâté from the northern
port city of Rouen says, "It was such a good duck."

PETIT-BEURRE
Etendard

Marque Déposée

^ The woman on this large package of Etendard brand butter is wearing the colors of the French national flag, or *tricolore,* as wildflowers in her hair.

> This poster, illustrated by Pierre Fève from 1936, is a request from the Syndicate of Wholesale Merchants of Apples and Pears to "Eat French fruit."

CONSOMMEZ
DES FRUITS FRANÇAIS

le hareng de fécamp

IMP. CANIS.PARIS

COMITÉ DE PROPAGANDE POUR DÉVELOPPER
LA CONSOMMATION DU HARENG DE FÉCAMP

17, QUAI BÉRIGNY. FÉCAMP (Seine-Inférieure)

∧ A flyer from the Committee for the Promotion of the Consumption of Herring from Fécamp (a harbor city on the north coast of France with a herring trade that goes back to the 10th century).

> A poster for Graminol brand instant Flan Lyonnais (custard tart), illustrated by Bellenger: "What a delicious dessert!"

le
FLAN LYONNAIS

quel dessert exquis!..

C'est un produit **"GRAMINOL"**

CAMEMBERT FABRIQUÉ EN NORMANDIE
LE PIERROT A LA ROSE
FROMAGERIE D'AUDRIEU (Calvados)
40% MATIÈRE GRASSE

Labels on small packages of Camembert cheese from regional manufacturers.

< Pierrot with a Rose brand and Clairette brand.

CAMEMBERT SUPÉRIEUR
L.C.B.F.
45% MATIÈRE GRASSE
"CLAIRETTE"
FABRIQUÉ EN CHARENTE-MARITIME

> Pik Nik brand
and The Refined
Gourmet brand from
the *département,*
province, of
Vienne.

> Flying Saucer brand pasteurized Camembert and Sputnik brand cheese: "The cheese of the future."

> The Driver brand
Camembert from Vienne,
and Sémaphore brand
Camembert from the
Indre region of
central France.

Maurice Chevalier rose up from the French music-hall tradition, but his style of novelty music ultimately brought him more success in the United States. Pictured is sheet music for songs made popular by Maurice Chevalier in revues at the Casino de Paris.

^ Sheet music for an operetta performed by Alice Cocea and
Maurice Chevalier at the Théâtre des Bouffes Parisiens in 1921.

^ Sheet music for a "shimmy"
from the revue *Très Excitante*, 1925.

^ This 1926 sheet music cover was designed by René Magritte
during a period when he was working as a commercial designer
just before his success as a Surrealist painter in Paris in 1928.

Jazz, swing, Latin and traditional: France's eclectic taste in music on phonograph record labels from the 1930s and '40s.

∧ From flower seller to one of the most highly paid female entertainers
in the world, Mistinguett, star of the Folies Bergère and Moulin Rouge,
sings some of her later career hits on this 45 rpm record from Odéon.

Edith Piaf, the great French musical icon, sang with authority and passion until her death in 1963. On this 45 she sings a song about a group of elite French soldiers called *les grognards*.

ESRF 1135 Ⓜ

edith
PIAF

LES GROGNARDS
les prisons du roy

Columbia

∧ Cinémonde magazine for November 1929 features Mexican actress Lupe Velez.

∧ This cinema weekly features actress Meg Lemonnier, who is bringing her stage success *Un Soir de Réveillon* to the screen, October 1933.

> A special edition of *VU*, from December 1934, celebrates the movies and features four French stars. Clockwise from top left: Jules Raimu, Gaby Morlay, Annabella, and below, Charles Boyer.

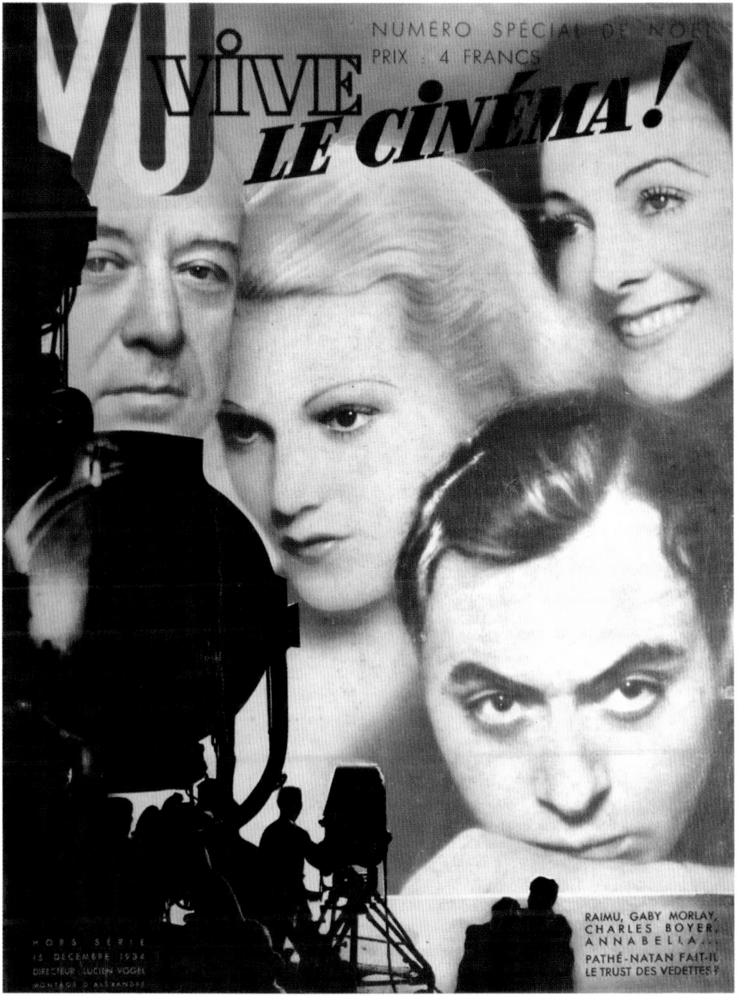

VU

VIVE
LE CINÉMA!

NUMÉRO SPÉCIAL DE NO[..]
PRIX : 4 FRANCS

RAIMU, GABY MORLAY,
CHARLES BOYER,
ANNABELLA...
PATHÉ-NATAN FAIT-IL
LE TRUST DES VEDETTES ?

HORS SÉRIE
15 DÉCEMBRE 1934
DIRECTEUR LUCIEN VOGEL
MONTAGE D'ALEXANDRE

LOCATION-FILM présente

la plus Belle du monde

^ This 1938 stage drama stars Véra Flory and was
directed by the Estonian immigrant filmmaker Dimitri Kirsanoff.

RAYMOND CORDY
JOSETTE DAY   ROBERT PIZANI ET
ANDRÉ BERLEY

DANS

SON
EXCELLENCE
ANTONIN

Scénario de **JEAN DEYRMON**
Adaptation et dialogue de **RENÉ PUJOL**
Réalisation de **C.F. TAVANO**

Lux COMPAGNIE CINÉMATOGRAPHIQUE de FRANCE . 26, rue de la Bienfaisance. PARIS . 62, rue St. Lazare. BRUXELLES

∧ The great character actor Raymond Cordy stars with Josette Day in the 1935 comedy *Son Excellence Antonin*, directed by Charles Tavano. Josette Day is best remembered as the star of Jean Cocteau's 1946 version of *Beauty and the Beast*.

SIRIUS

DANIEL GÉLIN
MARIA MAUBAN

RUMEUR PUBLIQUE

Un film de MAURIZIO CORGNATI
Adaptation et Dialogues de CHARLES SPAAK
AVEC
DELIA SCALA · MASSIMO SERATO · CARLO CAMPANINI · GIANRICO TEDESCHI

∧ After starring in this drama by director Maurizio Corgnati,
leading man Daniel Gélin went on to work with Max Ophüls,
Louis Malle, Jean Cocteau, and Alfred Hitchcock.

N° 241. - 7 Juillet 1935. 1 fr. Tous les Dimanches.

POLICE
MAGAZINE

fortes têtes
à pompon rouge

Lire, pages 8 et 9, le début d'une fort
intéressante enquête de Jean BAZAL
notre envoyé spécial à Toulon.

"The strong-headed man with a red pompom"—a trouble-making sailor—
the headline of the July 1935 edition of *Police Magazine*, about criminality
the Pigall area of Paris, then, as now, a neighborhood of dubious enterpris

^ This crime novel was written by Charles Ronze
and put out by Agence Parisienne de Distribution in 1941.

144

> Luggage labels from Paris hotels in the mid-twentieth century.

< Luggage labels from the Mediterranean cities of Nice and Marseille.

145

Luggage labels from
Paris, Tours, Lyon, and
Juan-Les-Pins on the Côte d'Azur.

147

^ Modernist designer Maximilian Vox created this advertisement in 1936 for a reduction in prices for weekend tickets on the "great networks" of the French railways.

CHEMINS DE FER DE L'ETAT
SOUTHERN RAILWAY

LONDRES

WATERLOO · VICTORIA

SOUTHAMPTON · NEWHAVEN

la nuit · le jour

LE HAVRE · DIEPPE

St LAZARE

PARIS

PARIS-VICHY
3ᴴ·49

EN AUTOMOTRICE **PLM** RAPIDE BUGATTI

J. B. Cⁱᵉ 1935

golden sands
blossoming orchards
and shaded groves
of
NORMANDY

L.SCRÉPEL
35

LES GRANDS RÉSEAUX FRANÇAIS ASSURENT

LE TRANSPORT
GRATUIT
DE VOTRE AUTOMOBILE

∧ The French state transportation network "offers free transport of your car" on its special car-carrying trains, states this poster from the 1930s.

‹ An English-language brochure for visitors to the "golden sands, blossoming orchards, and shaded groves of Normandy," illustrated by L. Scrépel, 1935.

French Line

Cᴵᵉ Gᴸᵉ TRANSATLANTIQUE

LISTE DES PASSAGERS

< The cabin & tourist class passenger list on the Le Havre to New York crossing of the French Line ship *Le Champlain*, July 9, 1932.

French Line

PIER 46 NORTH RIVER

NEW YORK

COMPAGNIE GÉNÉRALE TRANSATLANTIQUE
NEW YORK · LONDON · PARIS

French Line

Cᴵᵉ Gᴸᵉ

HAVRE SOUTHAMPTON NEW-YORK

TRANSATLANTIQUE

CABIN CLASS
BAGAGES DE CABINE

< ^ Luggage tags from The Compagnie Générale Transatlantique, known overseas as the French Line, whose great ocean liner fleet included the Déco masterpiece the *S.S. Normandie*.

In France, as well as throughout Europe, there was a tradition of commemorative stamps celebrating public events. In this case two trade fairs in Marseille (below) and Bicycle Week in Saint-Etienne in the 1930s (right).

SEMAINE DU CYCLE
du 2 au 9 NOVEMBRE
SAINT-ETIENNE
VELODROME D'HIVER

2e QUINZAINE DE SEPTEMBRE

FOIRE INTERNATIONALE DE MARSEILLE
MARCHE MEDITERRANEEN ET COLONIAL

MÉDITERRANÉENNE COLONIALE

FOIRE DE MARSEILLE
2ÈME QUINZAINE DE SEPTEMBRE

‹ ⌄ Two postage stamps
from the 1940s
exoticizing France's
colonial holdings.

Lottery tickets for the Loterie Indochinoise printed in Hanoi, Vietnam, the capital of the French Asian colonies in 1939, designed by G. Barrière.

MOT TRAM BAC · 壹百貫 · 東方滙理銀行 · 100

100

NGÂN-HÀNG QUỐC-GIA VIỆT-NAM
019820026
20 · 20
TỔNG KIỂM-TRA · THỦ-QUỸ TRUNG-ƯƠNG
HAI MƯƠI ĐỒNG
20026 · Z.8

東方滙理銀行 · 伍元
GIẤY NĂM ĐỒNG VÀNG

‹ ∧ The currency created by French designers and printers
for the Southeast Asian colonies, known as L'Indochine
Française, is considered by some collectors to be
among the most beautiful paper money ever made.
The bills here are from Cambodia, Vietnam, and Laos.

Throughout its history, Air France has produced posters
by significant artists, including "Extrême Orient" (above),
by Lucien Boucher, and "Afrique du Nord" (right),
by Bernard Villemot, 1948.

VU pioneered the concept of a bold, internationalist photo magazine and was the model for *Life* magazine in the United States. The logo for *VU* was designed by Leonetto Cappiello for its premier in 1928. These three issues from the early 1930s were devoted to world powers: "America Struggles" (left), "Inquiry into the Soviets" (below), and "France, the Country of Moderation" (right).

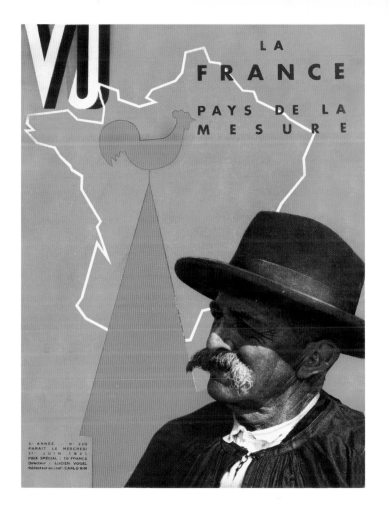

VU

5ᵉ ANNÉE   Nᵒ 220
PARAÎT LE MERCREDI
1ᵉʳ JUIN 1932
PRIX SPÉCIAL : 10 FRANCS
Directeur : LUCIEN VOGEL
Rédacteur en chef : CARLO RIM

LA
FRANCE
PAYS DE LA
MESURE

^ The board game *L'Autoroute: The Funny Road,* by Editions Dujardin, 1930s, imagines a car trip with a host of characters and misfortunes.

par économie
brûlez
du
coke

DE LA SOCIÉTÉ DU GAZ DE PARIS

^ A flyer for the Gas Company of Paris states
"For economy, burn coke."

> "The broom displaces dust, the vacuum cleaner removes it," says an
illustration promoting the use of electricity on this 1938 receipt for the
purchase of 140 kilowat-hours from Paris's electric company.

CTRICITÉ

–670

U

ES

S (6ᵉ Aʀ.)
7-10
STAL
NES)

TA

9. AOÛT 1938

Yves Guedon

LE BALAI
DÉPLACE LA POUSSIÈRE
L'ASPIRATEUR L'ABSORBE

JARACH Im

URENT AU CARNET D'ABONNÉ PLACÉ DERRIÈRE LE COMPT

our la période comprise et le nouveau relevé		timbres des contrats et avenants - déplacem' d'ouvrier - remplacem" de plombs - location de matériel - divers.	timbre (2) de quittance	MONTANT TO
	branchement ou colonne montante			
5	0300			13

CRÈME
IMPERMÉABLE POUR
CHAUSSURES

ALFRED

LE PINGOUIN

CRÈME·LAQUE
DE LUXE

MELITTA

ABBAYE ST. WANDRILLE S.I.

< A tin of Penguin brand waterproof cream for shoes (top), and a tin of Crème-Laque DeLuxe shoe polish (bottom).

< Three sheets of blotter paper with ads for shoe care products: Saphir Pate De Luxe renovating leather polish (top), Créme Éclipse with wax (middle), and Pingoline "cleans and bleaches all white leather" (bottom).

< *Miroir du Monde* rivaled *VU* magazine for topical stories, artistic photography, and experimental design. This cover (left), from April 1934 illustrates an article about the U.S.S.R. and Japan.

> The cover story for this 1936 issue of *Miroir du Monde* is titled "To the Ballot Box, RF [Republic of France]! Political and Economic Forces in France."

^ A fashionable aviator poses on the cover of the May 1936
issue of *Miroir du Monde,* which was devoted to vacations and tourism.

< A beauty ready for a day of boating is featured on this May 1939 cover of *Match*, "the weekly paper of international events," less than a year before the Nazi occupation and the institution of the collaborationist government of Marshal Philippe Pétain.

HEBDOMADAIRE DE L'ACTUALITÉ MONDIALE   4 MAI 1939   2^{fr}

> This issue of *Marie Claire* dates from its first year, 1937, when it was a weekly. Then, as now, it was a magazine of general interest for middle-class women.

LES JOIES DE L'HIVER   PRIX 1.

^ A curious mix of sewing, cooking tips, and social activism, in this issue
Femmes featured the Union for Peace, a group dedicated to causes ranging
from poverty in China to the Spanish Civil War (February 1939).

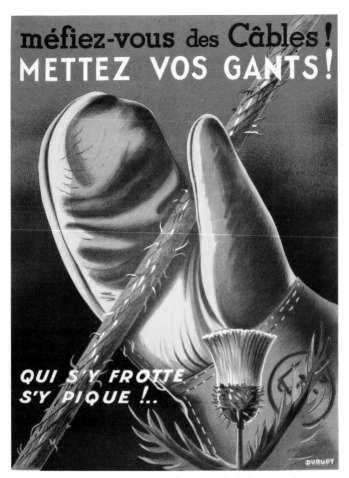

méfiez-vous des Câbles!
METTEZ VOS GANTS!

QUI S'Y FROTTE
S'Y PIQUE !..

DURUPT

^ Durupt, the illustrator of this safety poster for industrial workers,
used the image of a thistle to emphasize: "Be wary of cables,
put on your gloves!" to help avoid pricked fingers.

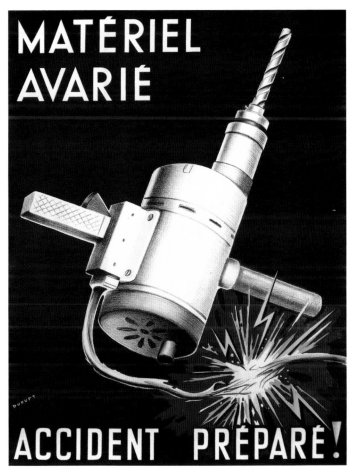

MATÉRIEL
AVARIÉ

ACCIDENT PRÉPARÉ!

^ This poster from the 1940s states, "Damaged tools lead to Accidents!"

A light Surrealist feel and a Post-Impressionist tone on two *Vogue* magazine covers; the vacation fashions of spring 1936 (above), and an illustration by Christian Bérard for the 1937 winter collections (right).

Vogue

Les Collections d'Hiver
Numéro Spécial
Octobre 1937
Prix 12 francs

REVUE MENSUELLE, LES ÉDITIONS CONDÉ NAST

VOGUE
SEPTEMBRE 1947
PRIX :
PUBLICATION BIMESTRIELLE IMPRIMÉE EN FRANCE
PRIX :
SEPTEMBRE 1947
VOGUE

< A pair of high-heel shoes from the 1940s with gold lamé wrapping, by an unnamed manufacturer.

< The design on this September 1947 cover of *Vogue* devoted to fall fashion, evokes a playing card.

> A bottle of Shanghai cologne by Lenthéric, from the 1940s.

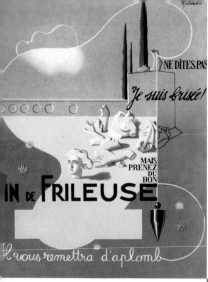

NE DÎTES PAS

Je suis brisée!

MAIS
PRENEZ
DU
BON

IN DE FRILEUSE

Il vous remettra d'aplomb

> Elsa Schiaparelli rivaled Coco Chanel as the most important fashion designer in Paris. In the 1930s she created a perfume based on the color pink, called "Shocking," advertised here with an illustration by her collaborator Marcel Vertes.

^ > Attempts to apply the iconography of Surrealism to advertising achieved mixed degrees of success. A "broken" woman is restored by Vin De Frileuse, 1938 (above), and a flower bursts into flame for a Guerlain perfume ad by the celebrated graphic designer A. M. Cassandre, 1952 (right).

Guerlain

PARFUMEUR A PARIS

Shocking

Cologne

Parfum

Schiaparelli

verti.

^ A downscale magazine called *V* flourished in the late 1940s
with tabloid-like stories. The March 1947 headline "Forbidden
to Women" refers to life in a monastery.

^ The January 1946 issue of *V* offers "A pretty smile to begin the year" and articles about the seamier side of London at night.

^ On the 1950 cover of this magazine of illustrated romance
stories, the heroine has fallen for a Montmartre-style
bohemian artist with a dubious variety of painting styles.

^ In this photo-Illustrated story from a 1953 issue of *Nous Deux*,
Eve has decisions to make after a day at the pool in Monte Carlo.

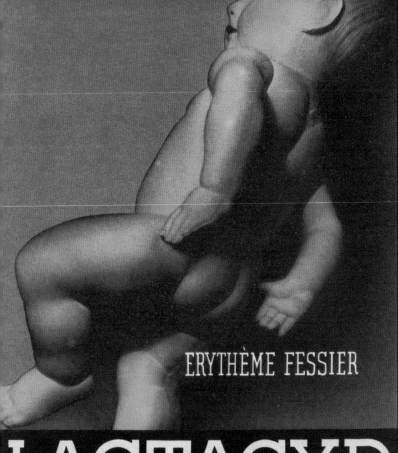

L'ACIDIFICATION EN DERMATOLOGIE

ERYTHÈME FESSIER

LACTACYD

PÂTE ANASEPTIQUE VITAMINÉE ACIDE $pH: 5,2$

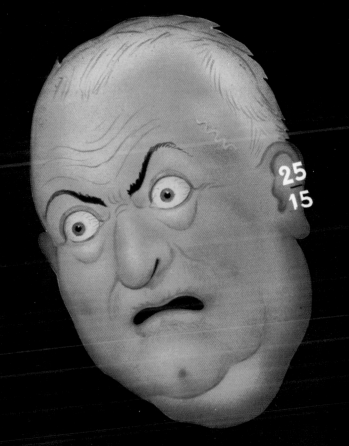

25
15

SEDANGOR

hypertension

PREVIOUS PAGE: A mailer advertising Lactacyd,
a medicated cream for diaper rash (left), and a mailer showing a
man in need of the hypertension medication Sedangor (right).

∧ A graphic representation of the beneficial
actions of Rhinofluine nasal decongestant.

> ∧ "It's time for a change," declares a revolutionary figure called a *sans-culotte,* with the traditional red hat, on a lithographed advertising flyer. "The only remedy: King brand wallpaper, will make your house look nicer."

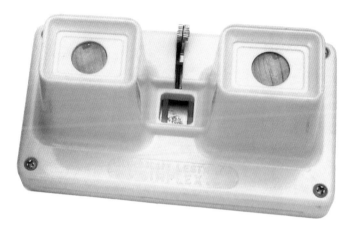

< ^ Two stereoviewer souvenirs of the Catholic pilgrimage site of
Lourdes in southern France; the "Stereoclic Super" by Bruguiere (left),
and the "Simplex" model from Lestrade Stereoscopes (above).

quinquina

In 1945, designer Werner Häschler created a successful
ad campaign for Saint-Raphaël's Quinquina aperitif
by manipulating a very distinctive visual formula.
These examples are from the mid-1950s.

Cigarette packages from the state tobacco
monopoly, Régie Française, including the famous Gitanes
brand (above) whose blue dancer design dates from 1943,
and De Troupe (opposite top) and Balto, "American Blend"
(opposite bottom) brands.

20 CIGARETTES

DE
TROUPE

G

BALTO

< ^ From 1937 until the 1960s the Photax camera company in Vitry-sur-Seine, near Paris, made a sleek Bakelite plastic camera, that became a much imitated classic for the casual camera user. The 1940s model above was called Blindé, armored, because of its Bakelite lens cap. The box at left is for a similar model.

^ An economical little camera called Top with its original box from the 1950s.

< A package of developed film from the town of Bazas in south-west France near the Atlantic coast.

^ The May 1936 issue of *La Science et la Vie* (above left) makes a prediction about a future source of electrical power; a car of the future that runs on atomic power is featured on the cover of *Science et Techniques Pour Tous*, December 1947 (above right).

^ A build-it-yourself radio kit called the
TransTronic Super 60 by Jouef, 1960.

LES CARNETS DU · COMMANDANT RENÉ ·

ÉCHEC À LA MONDAINE

ANDRÉ MARTEL

> France has had an affinity for mystery, police, and espionage novels since the beginning of the century. This novel by Tristan Bernard, was published in 1932 by Les Editions de France.

6 fr. LE LIVRE D'AUJOURD'HUI

TRISTAN BERNARD

AMANTS ET VOLEURS

LES EDITIONS DE FRANCE
20 AVENUE RAPP - PARIS

< This novel from the series The Files of Commander René, was published by André Martel in 1955.

TRANCHE DE VIE

LA MYSTÈRE

PRESSES DE LA CITÉ

RAE FOLEY

JEAN.PIERRE CONTY

ESPIONNAGE

Mr SUZUKI a des EMOTIONS FORTES

Editions "FLEUVE NOIR"

A. SAINT MOORE

DERNIER COLLIER pour DAME SEULE

.' SPECIAL POLICE '.

Editions "FLEUVE NOIR"

DIX MILLIONS DE TÉMOINS

PAR MICHELINE SANDREL

^ This adventure for "Zodiaque" was published
by Les Editions de Neuilly, 1956.

< French thrillers and romances catered to a range
of readers in the late 1950s and early 1960s.

^ A mechanical assassin menaces
the hero of this 1954 novel.

^ A showgirl is threatened by a snake in
this 1958 story from the series *Allo, Police*.

> A woman is saved by Bengali, the Dispenser of Justice, in this 1950s comic book.

< *Astrotomic,* a monthly comic book from 1948, resumes a science-fiction story called "S.O.S. Captain Vega."

^ "We are the construction workers, both future and present" proclaims this blotter paper offered by the Central Committee for the Coordination of Apprenticeships of Construction and Public Works announcing information on training.

Small bags with ads printed on them for "Trim Sport" track suits (left) and for Picardy's "Famous" table wine, "A Faithful Reflection of the Vine" (above).

La Dauphine by Renault

RENAULT
RÉGIE NATIONALE

FRANCE

owner's manual

∧ A 1959 owner's manual in English for the compact car La Dauphine (The Princess) by the Renault Régie Nationale, France, which stated that the car had the "simple beauty of a lady who doesn't have to wear jewels to prove her beauty."

> Blotter paper was a common piece of free mid-century advertising. These samples feature a Citroën truck on an ad for Mokaden Cafés (top) and a Panhard sports car on an ad for Grison "products for the care and maintainance of footwear" (bottom).

CITROËN 2CV

CAFÉS

Mokaden

I.P.A.M. - Schiryn/-Marne

D.B. PANHARD

Constituez votre
Collection avec les
différents modèles
de notre série :
"Automobiles"

Grison

TOUS LES PRODUITS D'ENTRETIEN POUR TOUTES CHAUSSURES

BUVARD NECTAR - CHARMEMENT

‹ ⌄ The idea of *Verve*, created by Efstratios Tériade, was to produce "the most beautiful magazine on Earth," using great artists of the day and including actual lithographic prints. The cover of the premier issue in 1937 was by Henri Matisse (left) and the second issue (1938) had a cover by Georges Braque (below).

∧ > In the 1960s, Livre de Poche published several of Jean Cocteau's novels printed with his own cover illustrations. Clockwise from top left: *Opéra*, *La Machine Infernale*, and *Les Enfants Terribles*.

> ❯ ❮ This deluxe portfolio of serigraph prints by artist Jean Picart le Doux was issued in 1956 to commemorate the centennial of the Compagnie de Pont-à-Mousson, makers of industrial water pipes. The style reflects late Surrealism and the collection has an introduction by artist Jean Cocteau.

< ∧ The art term "School of Paris" was loosely used to describe Post-Impressionists between the World Wars who employed Cubism, Surrealism, and Dada. After the Second World War the phrase often referred to a group of Post-Cubists working toward more abstract styles, as on these two gallery posters for shows by Dubuffet and LaGrange.

^ A stylized image of the Seine and the Île de la Cité
in Paris on a poster for Air France from the 1960s.

> The Compagnie Maritime des Chargeurs Réunis,
a shipping company, produced this poster in the 1950s,
showing one of their ships behind a calendar-style beauty.

^ "School of Paris" artist Raoul Dufy illustrated the cover of
the travel brochure "Paris: Where, What, When, How"
for the Comité de Tourisme de Paris in the 1950s.

∧ A brochure intended to encourage tourism immediately after World War II, published by the Ministry of Public Works and Transportation.

^The record album Plaisir des Dieux (Pleasure of the Gods), featuring bawdy songs performed by the Symphonie Bretonne, was issued for the workers of the Paris medical corps at a special annual party. The street scene on the cover is by Anri Ubair.

^ A seriograph poster from the 1950s for a dance band called Junior Club.

Elegant tabletop radios from the 1950s. Model RA-26U by Radiola (above) with a tuning dial that locates the cities and towns of Europe as well as Morocco and Algeria, the "Surcouf" by Oceanic (opposite top) has a green "bow" that lights up dramatically when playing; the "Excelsior 55" by Société Nouvelle Radio, 1954 (opposite bottom) glows with its "magic eye" and dual mirrored dials.

^ A collection of party records from the 1950s and '60s, including (clockwise from top left): Jazz favorites of Sidney Bechet, with Claude Luter; a comedy record by Jean Rigaux; *Riviera Danse,* by Los Maracaibos and their Brazilian Orchestra; and an album from the "Suprise Party" series with the orchestra of Jeff W. Higginbothom and Archie X. Morrisson.

> Two singers whose careers began in the French music-hall tradition of the 1930s and continued successfully into the postwar years: Charles Trenet, nicknamed "the singing madman" for his exuberant style (top), and Gilbert Bécaud, known as "Monsieur 100,000 Volts" for his intense stage presence (bottom).

^ The cover of this student theme book illustrates how a
record player provides "joy and comfort in the home."

^ Teppaz record players "bring joy" to the world, states this store sign from 1962.

< A Teppaz portable record player called "Oscar," made in Lyon in the early 1960s.

^ *Sonorama,* the magazine you could play on your record player, ran from 1958 to 1962. The first issue contained a speech by Charles de Gaulle and music by Gilbert Bécaud and by The Platters.

∧ > Issue number 23 of *Sonorama* (October, 1960) includes actress Brigitte Bardot's "hour of truth," news from the Congo, and music by Jean-Claude Pascal, "the last romantic of song."

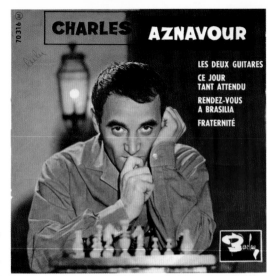

CHARLES AZNAVOUR

70316

LES DEUX GUITARES

CE JOUR
TANT ATTENDU

RENDEZ-VOUS
A BRASILIA

FRATERNITÉ

> Both Charles Aznavour (top)—the "Frank Sinatra of France"—and iconic crooner and actor Yves Montand (bottom) were said to have been "discovered" by Edith Piaf.

YVES MONTAND

PLANTER CAFÉ
Eddy Marnay — Emile Stern

MON MANÈGE
À MOI
J. Constantin — N. Glanzberg

RENDEZ-VOUS
DE PANAME
Francis Lemarque

ODEON
MOE 2153
MEDIUM

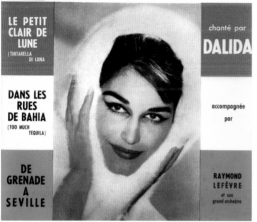

ROMANTICA

GRAND PRIX DE LA CHANSON ITALIENNE DU FESTIVAL DE SAN REMO 1960

LE PETIT
CLAIR DE
LUNE
(TINTARELLA
DI LUNA)

chanté par

DALIDA

DANS LES
RUES
DE BAHIA
(TOO MUCH
TEQUILA)

accompagnée
par

DE
GRENADE
A
SEVILLE

RAYMOND
LEFÈVRE
et son
grand orchestre

< Dalida, an Italian-Egyptian-French chanteuse, produced hit records from the 1950s into the disco era.

< Mireille Mathieu began singing pop hits in the mid-'60s, when she was called the new Edith Piaf for her rich voice.

70.996 M

pourquoi
mon amour

messieurs
les musiciens

le funambule

qu'elle est belle

mireille
mathieu

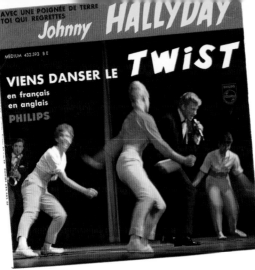

AVEC UNE POIGNÉE DE TERRE
TOI QUI REGRETTES

Johnny HALLYDAY

MEDIUM 432.593 B E

VIENS DANSER LE TWIST

en français
en anglais

PHILIPS

< Johnny Hallyday, one of France's most enduring rock stars, sang everything from '60s dance hits to gravel-voiced rock anthems.

> A pop-rock 45 titled *Crazy Mister Badge* by Eric Channe and his orchestra. The lyrics ask if Mr. Badge is insane or whether it's the "naked truth."

CRAZY MISTER BADGE

Premier prix EUROSCHNAFT 196jet

L'ARGENT NE FAIT PAS LE BONHEUR
LE TUNNEL SOUS LA MANCHE

LES VOLEURS DU TRAIN POSTAL
ON PARLE AVEC LES MAINS

M 437 242 BE

LES PARISIENNES

ET CLAUDE BOLLING

PHILIPS

PHILIPS

^ This 45 by choral pop group Les Parisiennes from
the 1960s is typically fashionable for its era.

force
énergie
santé...

avec les *MIELS*
Rémond
PURS NATURELS SÉLECTIONNÉS

CAHIER DE _____

appartenant à _____

^ An ad touting "strength, energy, and health, with Rémond brand Honey" appears on a student notebook.

> Since 1925, the helmet of a Gallic warrior in a blue disc has given its name to one of France's most popular cigarettes, Gauloises. This poster by Henri Faure is from the mid-'50s.

DISQUE BLEU

RÉGIE FRANÇAISE DES TABACS · CAISSE AUTONOME D'AMORTISSEMENT

∧ This poster from the 1980s for the Loterie Nationale, illustrated by Fassianos, suggests offering a lottery ticket for Father's Day.

‹ French decorators have always had a special fondness for spectacular wallpaper. These two 1960s prototypes are from an unnamed design studio in Lyon.

^ A program from the Jacki Clérico and Roland Léonar production
of *Frénésie* at the Moulin Rouge in the early 1980s.

sans hésiter

le rouge baiser

CALCULÉ A PARIS PAR PAUL BAUDECROUX

LE ROUGE UNIQUE PAR SA QUALITÉ DE CLASSE MONDIALE

^ "Without hesitation: The Red Kiss," an ad for lipstick illustrated by René Gruau. Le Rouge Baiser brand was created by Paul Baudecroux, a pioneer in lipstick chemistry and marketing.

235

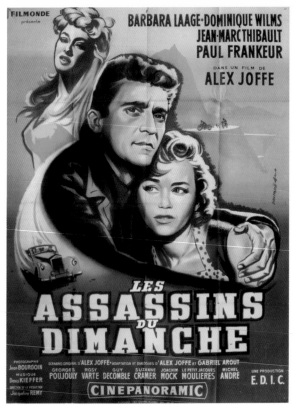

^ *Les Assassins du Dimanche*, a film by Alex Joffe presented
by Filmonde, was made in 1956. Actor Paul Frankeur also appeared
in films by Jacques Tati and Luis Buñuel.

> *Des Frissons Partout* starred Eddie Constantine, a Los Angeles
immigrant who became a cult star acting in French B movies in the 1950s
as secret agent Lemmy Caution. He played a reprised version of that
character in Jean-Luc Godard's *Alphaville* in 1965.

EDDIE CONSTANTINE

DES FRISSONS PARTOUT

Un Film de **RAOUL ANDRÉ** avec **PERRETTE PRADIER** et **DANIEL EMILFORK**

JEAN GALLAND — PAUL BONIFAS — DAPHNÉ DAYLE — SOPHIE HARDY — JEAN·JACQUES STEEN — GISÈLE ROBERT

CLÉMENT HARARI avec **JANINE VILA** et **NANDO GAZZOLO** SCÉNARIO ET DIALOGUE DE **MICHEL LEBRUN**

MUSIQUE DE MICHEL MAGNE · · · · · · · publicité J. Koutachy, paris · · · · · · UNE COPRODUCTION FRANCO-ITALIENNE LES PRODUCTIONS JACQUES ROITFELD · Paris · FIDA CINÉMATOGRAFICA · Rome

Play Time

un film de jacques tati

∧ Great comedic film star and director Jacques Tati made his first major film, *Jour de Fête,* as a tribute to small-town French life in 1949. This poster, illustrated by Landi, was for a later rerelease.

< *Playtime,* Jacques Tati's most ambitious and expensive film, was a critique of the transformation of Paris into an Americanized glass-and-steel disaster. Nine years in the making, it was released in 1967.

^ The April 1959 edition of *Cinémonde* magazine was devoted to the Cannes Film Festival and featured actress Annette Vadim, star of *Les Liaisons Dangereuses*. François Truffaut's *Les Quatre Cents Coups*, one of the defining films of the French New Wave, was France's lead entry that year.

> *Terrain Vague,* from 1960, was a late work by the master of "poetic realism" Marcel Carné, whose most memorable film was 1945's *Les Enfants du Paradis*.

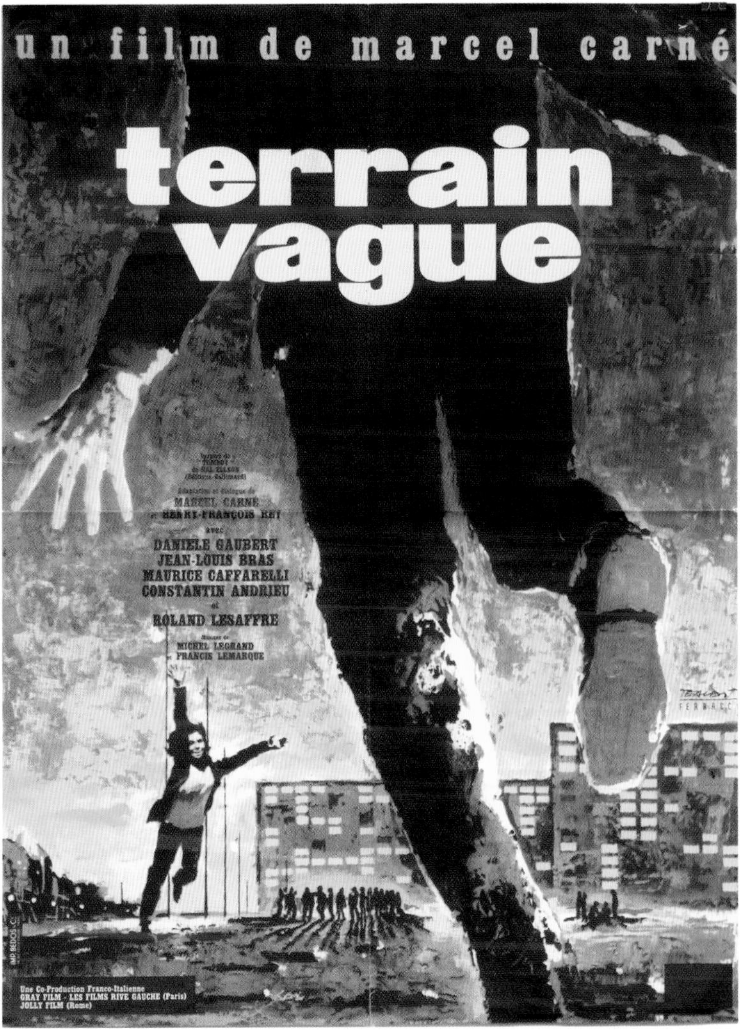

un film de marcel carné
terrain vague
avec
DANIELE GAUBERT
JEAN-LOUIS BRAS
MAURICE CAFFARELLI
CONSTANTIN ANDRIEU
ROLAND LESAFFRE
MICHEL LEGRAND
FRANCIS LEMARQUE
Une Co-Production Franco-Italienne
GRAY FILM - LES FILMS RIVE GAUCHE (Paris)
JOLLY FILM (Rome)

< ^ In the influential film magazine *Cahiers Du Cinéma*, François Truffaut, Jean-Luc Godard, and many others formulated the iconoclastic theories that formed the burst of cinematic creativity called the French New Wave. These issues from the early 1960s feature articles on Jerry Lewis, Ingmar Bergman, and Léonard Keigel.

> Jean-Luc Godard's 1963 film *Le Mépris,* starring Brigitte Bardot and Jack Palance, positioned these two stars in a critique of the film industry.

^ Jean-Luc Godard's 1965 film starring Jean-Paul Belmondo and Anna Karina was a gangster movie with a pop art aesthetic that became a critical and financial success.

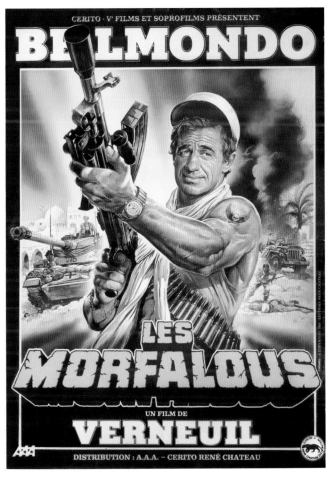

^ By 1984, Jean-Paul Belmondo had become a mainstream commercial star, often playing in comedies or in the role of cynical heroes.

LA PLANETE
SAUVAGE

ファンタスティック・プラネット

ローラン・トポールの
怪奇と幻想にみちたイメージ

LA PLANETE SAUVAGE
Un film de RENE LALOUX
Scénario et dialogue ROLAND TOPOR, RENE LALOUX
d'après le roman de Stefan WUL, OMS EN SERIE
Dessins originaux ROLAND TOPOR
Directeurs du dessin animé JOSEPH KABRT, JOSEPH VANA
Musique Alain GORAGUER Arrangements JEAN GUERIN
Co-production LES FILMS ARMORIAL, ORTF, PARIS
CESKOSLOVENSKY FILMEXPORT PRAGUE
Distribution by Cable Hogue

∧ The magazine *Métal Hurlant* (literally "Howling Metal")
began in 1974 and was a groundbreaking combination
of science fiction, horror, sex, and underground comics.

< *La Planète Sauvage* (Fantastic Planet), an animated
science-fiction film directed by René Laloux in 1973, had
a Surrealistic graphic style that was influential worldwide.
This poster is for the Japanese release.

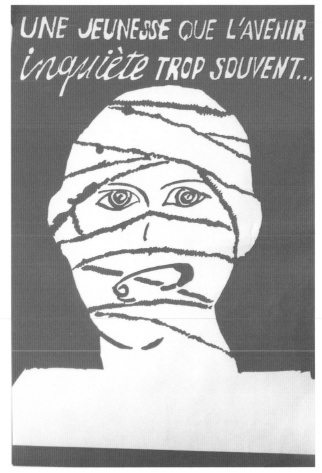

^ The student protests and the massive general strikes of May 1968, which caused the eventual collapse of the De Gaulle government, produced graphic posters like this one showing "Young people who are scared about the future."

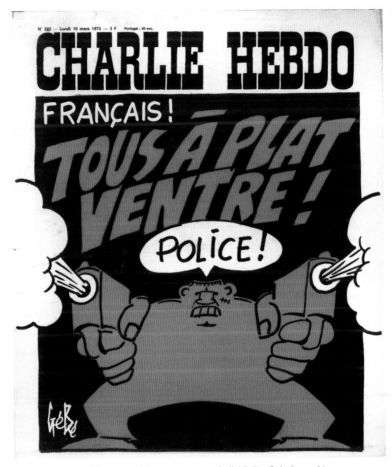

^ "Frenchmen! Everyone on your belly! Police!" declares this
cover for March 1975 of *Charlie Hebdo*, a leftist, anarchist
newspaper whose irreverent tone is reminiscent of the weeklies
from the beginning of the twentieth century.

SUPERHEBDO

L'ETONNANTE
CONFESSION DE
FRANÇOISE
HARDY
VOIR PAGE 2

3

250

< ^ Two psychedelic covers of *Superhebdo*, a paper of rock music and pop culture from 1970. The cover at left was designed by Beruard Envard; the cover above was uncredited.

B A Z O O K A

FRANÇAIS–ANGLAIS · ENGLISH–FRENCH

Bulletin
périodique

Dissimulation en ambiances
particulières · Dissimulation
in particular environment

int–18 ans

NO 7
10 fr

UK1£·Belg100fr·

1978

C A M O U F L A G E

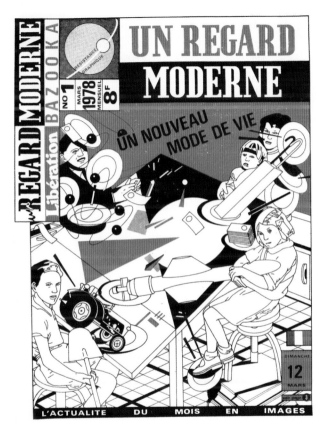

^ < Bazooka was a group of designers dedicated to a leftist and punk aesthetic who produced a large namesake magazine filled with Constructivist and mostly wordless visual commentary on contemporary subjects. At left, issue number 7 from 1978; above, a magazine by Bazooka, commissioned by the newspaper *Libération* in March 1978.

Credits

Most items are from the author's collection, with these generous exceptions:

Pages 37 (purse) and 177 (shoes): Courtesy of Pammela Springfield at Keep 'Em Flying, Portland Oregon.

Pages 46 and 48: Fashion prints courtesy Eugene E. Mitchell.

Pages 57 (radio and speaker), 68 (ad), 197 (radio set), and 223 (ad and phonograph) very generously provided by Jean-Luc Fradet, www.tsf36.com, Déols, France.

Pages 69 (camera), 194 (camera box), 195 (box and camera) and 188 and 189 (stereoviewers with boxes): Courtesy of Régis Boissier at candidcamera.free.fr, Lyon, France.

^ A decorative stamp from the Touring Club of France, *"The Most Beautiful Country in the World."*

Pages 80 and 150: Brochures courtesy of Elisabeth Burdon at oldimprints.com.

Page 87: Cigarette box from the collection of Yves Edmond Le Meitour, Le Meitour Gallery, Portland, Oregon.

Pages 218 and 219: The three radios were photographed courtesy of Merrill L. Mabbs, ClassicRadioGallery.com, from his extraordinary collection, Rapid City, South Dakota.

Acknowledgments

The author would like to thank the many people who made this little book possible:

First and foremost, the late Édouard Pécourt, for the collection of ephemera from his country of birth and for his charming anecdotes and insights, and his wife Jocelyn Howells.

Elisabeth Burdon, Dana Hoyle, Yves Edmond Le Meitour, and Pammela Springfield for their kind indulgences.

Bernard Sampo for his translations and cultural insight.

Moto Hyun for his travel companionship, and the many generous personalities at the flea markets of Saint-Ouen and Porte de Vanves in Paris, and also the *bouquinistes* along the Seine.

Steve Mockus at Chronicle Books for his trust and enthusiasm.

And Morgan Cha for his support.

‹ Bibendum, the Michelin Man, has been the trademark of the Michelin Tire Manufacturing Company of France since 1898. This is a squeak toy from the 1980s.

NEXT PAGE: Art from a guide map for the Exposition Internationale, 1937, distributed courtesy of Bon Marché department stores, Paris.